# 50 Diabetic Delights
# Recipes for Home

By: Kelly Johnson

## Table of Contents

- Grilled Lemon Herb Chicken
- Zucchini Noodles with Pesto
- Quinoa and Black Bean Salad
- Cauliflower Rice Stir-Fry
- Baked Salmon with Asparagus
- Spinach and Feta Stuffed Chicken Breast
- Roasted Vegetable Medley
- Turkey and Spinach Lettuce Wraps
- Stuffed Bell Peppers with Quinoa
- Chia Seed Pudding with Berries
- Eggplant Parmesan (Baked)
- Mediterranean Chickpea Salad
- Low-Carb Chicken Enchiladas
- Shrimp Tacos with Cabbage Slaw
- Sweet Potato and Black Bean Chili
- Greek Yogurt Parfait with Nuts
- Almond Flour Pancakes
- Savory Oatmeal with Spinach and Egg
- Coconut Curry Lentil Soup
- Grilled Vegetable Skewers
- Spaghetti Squash with Marinara
- Herb-Roasted Chicken Thighs
- Avocado and Tomato Salad
- Mushroom and Spinach Frittata
- Baked Tilapia with Lemon and Dill
- Low-Carb Pizza with Cauliflower Crust
- Lentil and Vegetable Stew
- Greek Salad with Grilled Chicken
- Coconut Flour Muffins
- Cabbage Roll Casserole
- Berry Smoothie with Spinach
- Oven-Baked Falafel
- Almond-Crusted Chicken Tenders
- Roasted Brussels Sprouts with Balsamic
- Curried Quinoa and Vegetable Bowl

- Zesty Lemon Garlic Shrimp
- Apple Cinnamon Overnight Oats
- Beef and Broccoli Stir-Fry
- Cilantro Lime Rice with Black Beans
- Creamy Avocado Dressing Salad
- Herb-Crusted Baked Cod
- Spiced Chickpeas and Spinach
- Green Bean Almondine
- Low-Sugar Chocolate Avocado Mousse
- Baked Acorn Squash with Cinnamon
- Spicy Roasted Cauliflower
- Mediterranean Stuffed Zucchini
- Grilled Eggplant with Tomato Sauce
- Raspberry Chia Jam
- Nutty Granola Bars (Low-Sugar)

# Grilled Lemon Herb Chicken

**Ingredients**

- 4 boneless, skinless chicken breasts
- 1/4 cup olive oil
- Juice of 2 lemons
- Zest of 1 lemon
- 3 cloves garlic, minced
- 1 tablespoon fresh rosemary, chopped (or 1 teaspoon dried)
- 1 tablespoon fresh thyme, chopped (or 1 teaspoon dried)
- 1 teaspoon salt
- 1/2 teaspoon black pepper
- 1/2 teaspoon red pepper flakes (optional)

**Instructions**

1. **Marinate the Chicken:**
    - In a bowl, whisk together olive oil, lemon juice, lemon zest, garlic, rosemary, thyme, salt, pepper, and red pepper flakes.
    - Place the chicken breasts in a resealable plastic bag or shallow dish. Pour the marinade over the chicken, ensuring it's well coated. Seal the bag or cover the dish, and refrigerate for at least 30 minutes (up to 4 hours for more flavor).
2. **Preheat the Grill:**
    - Preheat your grill to medium-high heat (about 375°F to 400°F).
3. **Grill the Chicken:**
    - Remove the chicken from the marinade and let excess marinade drip off. Discard the marinade.
    - Place the chicken on the grill. Cook for about 6-7 minutes on one side, then flip and cook for another 5-6 minutes, or until the internal temperature reaches 165°F (75°C) and the chicken is cooked through.
4. **Rest and Serve:**
    - Remove the chicken from the grill and let it rest for 5 minutes before slicing. This helps keep it juicy.
    - Serve with additional lemon wedges and your favorite side dishes, such as grilled vegetables or a fresh salad.

**Tips**

- For added flavor, you can baste the chicken with the marinade during grilling (make sure it's cooked first if you do).
- Pair this dish with a light white wine, like Sauvignon Blanc, for a refreshing meal.

Enjoy your delicious grilled lemon herb chicken!

## Zucchini Noodles with Pesto

**Ingredients**

- 4 medium zucchinis
- 1 cup fresh basil leaves
- 1/2 cup grated Parmesan cheese
- 1/3 cup pine nuts (or walnuts)
- 2 cloves garlic
- 1/2 cup olive oil
- Salt and pepper to taste
- Cherry tomatoes, halved (for garnish, optional)

**Instructions**

1. **Make the Pesto:**
   - In a food processor, combine basil, Parmesan, pine nuts, garlic, and a pinch of salt and pepper. Pulse until finely chopped.
   - With the processor running, slowly drizzle in the olive oil until smooth.
2. **Prepare the Zucchini Noodles:**
   - Using a spiralizer or a vegetable peeler, create zucchini noodles.
3. **Combine:**
   - In a large skillet over medium heat, add the zucchini noodles and sauté for 2-3 minutes until just tender.
   - Remove from heat and toss with the pesto until evenly coated.
4. **Serve:**
   - Garnish with cherry tomatoes and additional Parmesan, if desired.

## Quinoa and Black Bean Salad

**Ingredients**

- 1 cup quinoa
- 2 cups water or vegetable broth
- 1 can (15 oz) black beans, rinsed and drained
- 1 bell pepper (red or yellow), diced
- 1 cup corn (fresh, frozen, or canned)
- 1/4 cup red onion, finely chopped
- 1/4 cup fresh cilantro, chopped
- Juice of 2 limes
- 2 tablespoons olive oil
- Salt and pepper to taste

**Instructions**

1. **Cook the Quinoa:**
    - Rinse quinoa under cold water. In a saucepan, combine quinoa and water/broth. Bring to a boil, then reduce heat, cover, and simmer for about 15 minutes or until quinoa is fluffy. Let it cool.
2. **Combine Ingredients:**
    - In a large bowl, combine the cooled quinoa, black beans, bell pepper, corn, red onion, and cilantro.
3. **Dress the Salad:**
    - In a small bowl, whisk together lime juice, olive oil, salt, and pepper. Pour over the salad and toss to combine.
4. **Serve:**
    - Chill for at least 30 minutes before serving to let the flavors meld.

# Cauliflower Rice Stir-Fry

**Ingredients**

- 1 medium head of cauliflower
- 2 tablespoons vegetable oil
- 3 cloves garlic, minced
- 1 cup mixed vegetables (carrots, peas, bell peppers)
- 2 eggs, beaten (optional)
- 3 tablespoons soy sauce
- 1 tablespoon sesame oil
- 2 green onions, sliced
- Salt and pepper to taste

**Instructions**

1. **Prepare Cauliflower Rice:**
   - Remove leaves and stem from the cauliflower. Cut it into florets and pulse in a food processor until it resembles rice.
2. **Stir-Fry:**
   - Heat vegetable oil in a large skillet or wok over medium heat. Add minced garlic and sauté for 30 seconds.
   - Add mixed vegetables and stir-fry for about 3-5 minutes until tender.
3. **Add Cauliflower Rice:**
   - Stir in the cauliflower rice and cook for an additional 5-7 minutes until softened.
4. **Incorporate Eggs (Optional):**
   - Push the rice to one side of the pan, pour in the beaten eggs, and scramble until fully cooked. Mix into the rice.
5. **Season:**
   - Add soy sauce and sesame oil, mixing well. Season with salt and pepper to taste.
6. **Serve:**
   - Garnish with sliced green onions before serving.

Enjoy your delicious and healthy meals!

# Baked Salmon with Asparagus

## Ingredients

- 4 salmon fillets
- 1 bunch asparagus, trimmed
- 2 tablespoons olive oil
- Juice of 1 lemon
- 2 cloves garlic, minced
- Salt and pepper to taste
- 1 teaspoon dried oregano (optional)

## Instructions

1. **Preheat the Oven:**
    - Preheat your oven to 400°F (200°C).
2. **Prepare the Dish:**
    - On a baking sheet, arrange salmon fillets and asparagus. Drizzle with olive oil and lemon juice. Sprinkle with garlic, salt, pepper, and oregano.
3. **Bake:**
    - Bake for 12-15 minutes, or until the salmon is cooked through and flakes easily with a fork.
4. **Serve:**
    - Serve immediately, garnished with lemon wedges if desired.

# Spinach and Feta Stuffed Chicken Breast

## Ingredients

- 4 boneless, skinless chicken breasts
- 2 cups fresh spinach, chopped
- 1 cup feta cheese, crumbled
- 2 cloves garlic, minced
- 1 tablespoon olive oil
- Salt and pepper to taste
- 1 teaspoon dried oregano

## Instructions

1. **Preheat the Oven:**
    - Preheat your oven to 375°F (190°C).
2. **Prepare the Filling:**
    - In a skillet, heat olive oil over medium heat. Add garlic and spinach, sautéing until wilted. Remove from heat and stir in feta, oregano, salt, and pepper.
3. **Stuff the Chicken:**
    - Cut a pocket into each chicken breast. Fill each pocket with the spinach and feta mixture.
4. **Bake:**
    - Place stuffed chicken breasts in a baking dish and bake for 25-30 minutes, or until cooked through.
5. **Serve:**
    - Let rest for a few minutes before slicing and serving.

# Roasted Vegetable Medley

**Ingredients**

- 2 cups broccoli florets
- 2 cups cauliflower florets
- 1 red bell pepper, chopped
- 1 zucchini, sliced
- 2 tablespoons olive oil
- Salt and pepper to taste
- 1 teaspoon garlic powder (optional)

**Instructions**

1. **Preheat the Oven:**
   - Preheat your oven to 425°F (220°C).
2. **Prepare the Vegetables:**
   - In a large bowl, toss all vegetables with olive oil, salt, pepper, and garlic powder.
3. **Roast:**
   - Spread the vegetables in a single layer on a baking sheet. Roast for 20-25 minutes, or until tender and slightly caramelized.
4. **Serve:**
   - Serve warm as a side dish.

# Turkey and Spinach Lettuce Wraps

## Ingredients

- 1 pound ground turkey
- 2 cups fresh spinach, chopped
- 2 cloves garlic, minced
- 1 tablespoon soy sauce
- 1 tablespoon olive oil
- 1 teaspoon sesame oil (optional)
- Butter lettuce leaves (or any lettuce for wraps)
- Sliced green onions (for garnish)

## Instructions

1. **Cook the Turkey:**
    - In a skillet, heat olive oil over medium heat. Add garlic and sauté for 30 seconds, then add ground turkey and cook until browned.
2. **Add Spinach:**
    - Stir in spinach, soy sauce, and sesame oil. Cook until spinach is wilted.
3. **Serve:**
    - Spoon turkey mixture into lettuce leaves and garnish with green onions.

# Stuffed Bell Peppers with Quinoa

## Ingredients

- 4 bell peppers (any color)
- 1 cup cooked quinoa
- 1 can (15 oz) black beans, rinsed and drained
- 1 cup corn (fresh, frozen, or canned)
- 1 teaspoon cumin
- 1 teaspoon chili powder
- 1 cup salsa
- 1 cup shredded cheese (cheddar or Monterey Jack)

## Instructions

1. **Preheat the Oven:**
   - Preheat your oven to 375°F (190°C).
2. **Prepare the Peppers:**
   - Cut the tops off the bell peppers and remove seeds. Place them in a baking dish.
3. **Make the Filling:**
   - In a large bowl, mix cooked quinoa, black beans, corn, cumin, chili powder, and half of the salsa.
4. **Stuff the Peppers:**
   - Fill each bell pepper with the quinoa mixture. Top with the remaining salsa and cheese.
5. **Bake:**
   - Cover with foil and bake for 30 minutes. Remove foil and bake for an additional 10 minutes, or until the peppers are tender and cheese is melted.
6. **Serve:**
   - Let cool slightly before serving.

Enjoy your delicious meals!

# Chia Seed Pudding with Berries

## Ingredients

- 1/2 cup chia seeds
- 2 cups almond milk (or any milk of choice)
- 2 tablespoons maple syrup or honey
- 1 teaspoon vanilla extract
- 1 cup mixed berries (strawberries, blueberries, raspberries)
- Fresh mint (for garnish, optional)

## Instructions

1. **Prepare the Pudding:**
    - In a bowl, whisk together chia seeds, almond milk, maple syrup, and vanilla extract until well combined.
2. **Refrigerate:**
    - Cover and refrigerate for at least 4 hours or overnight until thickened.
3. **Serve:**
    - Spoon the pudding into bowls, top with mixed berries, and garnish with fresh mint if desired.

## Eggplant Parmesan (Baked)

**Ingredients**

- 2 medium eggplants, sliced
- 2 cups marinara sauce
- 2 cups mozzarella cheese, shredded
- 1 cup Parmesan cheese, grated
- 1 cup breadcrumbs (optional)
- 1 tablespoon olive oil
- 1 teaspoon Italian seasoning
- Salt and pepper to taste

**Instructions**

1. **Prepare the Eggplant:**
   - Preheat the oven to 375°F (190°C). Sprinkle eggplant slices with salt and let sit for 30 minutes to draw out moisture. Rinse and pat dry.
2. **Bake the Eggplant:**
   - Brush eggplant slices with olive oil and place on a baking sheet. Bake for 25 minutes until tender.
3. **Layer Ingredients:**
   - In a baking dish, layer marinara sauce, eggplant slices, mozzarella, and Parmesan. Repeat layers, finishing with cheese on top.
4. **Bake:**
   - Bake for 25-30 minutes until cheese is bubbly and golden. Let cool for a few minutes before serving.

## Mediterranean Chickpea Salad

### Ingredients

- 1 can (15 oz) chickpeas, rinsed and drained
- 1 cucumber, diced
- 1 cup cherry tomatoes, halved
- 1/4 red onion, finely chopped
- 1/2 cup Kalamata olives, pitted and sliced
- 1/4 cup feta cheese, crumbled
- 2 tablespoons olive oil
- Juice of 1 lemon
- Salt and pepper to taste
- Fresh parsley, chopped (for garnish)

### Instructions

1. **Combine Ingredients:**
    - In a large bowl, mix chickpeas, cucumber, cherry tomatoes, red onion, olives, and feta cheese.
2. **Dress the Salad:**
    - In a small bowl, whisk together olive oil, lemon juice, salt, and pepper. Pour over the salad and toss to combine.
3. **Serve:**
    - Garnish with fresh parsley before serving.

# Low-Carb Chicken Enchiladas

## Ingredients

- 2 cups shredded cooked chicken
- 1 cup shredded cheese (cheddar or Monterey Jack)
- 1 cup enchilada sauce
- 1/2 cup cream cheese, softened
- 1 teaspoon cumin
- 1 teaspoon chili powder
- Large lettuce leaves (for wrapping)

## Instructions

1. **Prepare the Filling:**
    - In a bowl, mix shredded chicken, cream cheese, cumin, chili powder, and half of the cheese.
2. **Assemble the Enchiladas:**
    - Spoon the chicken mixture into lettuce leaves and roll up. Place seam-side down in a baking dish.
3. **Top with Sauce:**
    - Pour enchilada sauce over the wrapped chicken and sprinkle with remaining cheese.
4. **Bake:**
    - Preheat the oven to 350°F (175°C) and bake for 15-20 minutes until cheese is melted and bubbly.

# Shrimp Tacos with Cabbage Slaw

## Ingredients

- 1 pound shrimp, peeled and deveined
- 1 tablespoon olive oil
- 1 teaspoon cumin
- 1 teaspoon chili powder
- Salt and pepper to taste
- 8 small corn or flour tortillas
- 2 cups green cabbage, shredded
- 1/4 cup cilantro, chopped
- Juice of 1 lime
- Avocado slices (for serving, optional)

## Instructions

1. **Cook the Shrimp:**
    - In a skillet, heat olive oil over medium heat. Add shrimp, cumin, chili powder, salt, and pepper. Cook until shrimp are pink and opaque, about 3-4 minutes.
2. **Prepare the Slaw:**
    - In a bowl, combine shredded cabbage, cilantro, lime juice, and a pinch of salt.
3. **Assemble Tacos:**
    - Warm tortillas and fill each with shrimp and cabbage slaw. Top with avocado slices if desired.
4. **Serve:**
    - Serve immediately with lime wedges on the side.

## Sweet Potato and Black Bean Chili

### Ingredients

- 2 medium sweet potatoes, diced
- 1 can (15 oz) black beans, rinsed and drained
- 1 can (14 oz) diced tomatoes
- 1 cup vegetable broth
- 1 onion, diced
- 2 cloves garlic, minced
- 1 tablespoon chili powder
- 1 teaspoon cumin
- Salt and pepper to taste
- Fresh cilantro (for garnish)

### Instructions

1. **Sauté Aromatics:**
   - In a large pot, sauté onion and garlic until soft.
2. **Add Ingredients:**
   - Add diced sweet potatoes, black beans, diced tomatoes, vegetable broth, chili powder, cumin, salt, and pepper.
3. **Simmer:**
   - Bring to a boil, then reduce heat and simmer for 20-25 minutes until sweet potatoes are tender.
4. **Serve:**
   - Garnish with fresh cilantro before serving.

Enjoy your delicious meals!

# Greek Yogurt Parfait with Nuts

## Ingredients

- 2 cups Greek yogurt
- 1 cup mixed berries (strawberries, blueberries, raspberries)
- 1/4 cup granola
- 1/4 cup nuts (almonds, walnuts, or pecans)
- Honey or maple syrup (for drizzling, optional)

## Instructions

1. **Layer Ingredients:**
   - In a glass or bowl, layer Greek yogurt, mixed berries, granola, and nuts.
2. **Drizzle:**
   - If desired, drizzle with honey or maple syrup.
3. **Serve:**
   - Enjoy immediately as a nutritious breakfast or snack.

# Almond Flour Pancakes

## Ingredients

- 1 cup almond flour
- 2 eggs
- 1/4 cup almond milk (or any milk of choice)
- 1 tablespoon honey or maple syrup
- 1 teaspoon baking powder
- 1/2 teaspoon vanilla extract
- Butter or oil (for cooking)

## Instructions

1. **Mix Ingredients:**
   - In a bowl, whisk together almond flour, eggs, almond milk, honey, baking powder, and vanilla until smooth.
2. **Cook Pancakes:**
   - Heat butter or oil in a skillet over medium heat. Pour batter to form pancakes and cook for 2-3 minutes per side until golden brown.
3. **Serve:**
   - Serve warm with your favorite toppings, such as fresh fruit or syrup.

## Savory Oatmeal with Spinach and Egg

**Ingredients**

- 1 cup rolled oats
- 2 cups vegetable broth or water
- 2 cups fresh spinach
- 2 eggs
- Salt and pepper to taste
- 1 tablespoon olive oil
- Grated Parmesan cheese (for topping, optional)

**Instructions**

1. **Cook Oats:**
    - In a saucepan, bring vegetable broth or water to a boil. Stir in oats, reduce heat, and simmer for about 5 minutes until cooked.
2. **Sauté Spinach:**
    - In a skillet, heat olive oil over medium heat. Add spinach and sauté until wilted. Season with salt and pepper.
3. **Cook Eggs:**
    - In the same skillet, cook eggs to your preference (fried or poached).
4. **Combine and Serve:**
    - Divide oatmeal into bowls, top with sautéed spinach and eggs, and sprinkle with Parmesan if desired.

# Coconut Curry Lentil Soup

## Ingredients

- 1 cup lentils (red or green)
- 1 can (14 oz) coconut milk
- 4 cups vegetable broth
- 1 onion, diced
- 2 cloves garlic, minced
- 1 tablespoon curry powder
- 1 teaspoon ginger, minced
- Salt and pepper to taste
- Fresh cilantro (for garnish)

## Instructions

1. **Sauté Aromatics:**
   - In a large pot, sauté onion and garlic until soft. Add ginger and curry powder, cooking for another minute.
2. **Add Lentils and Liquids:**
   - Stir in lentils, coconut milk, and vegetable broth. Bring to a boil, then reduce heat and simmer for 25-30 minutes until lentils are tender.
3. **Blend (Optional):**
   - For a creamier texture, blend part of the soup with an immersion blender.
4. **Serve:**
   - Season with salt and pepper, garnish with fresh cilantro, and serve warm.

# Grilled Vegetable Skewers

## Ingredients

- 1 zucchini, sliced
- 1 bell pepper, chopped
- 1 red onion, chopped
- 1 cup cherry tomatoes
- 2 tablespoons olive oil
- Salt and pepper to taste
- 1 teaspoon Italian seasoning

## Instructions

1. **Preheat Grill:**
   - Preheat your grill to medium heat.
2. **Prepare Skewers:**
   - In a bowl, toss vegetables with olive oil, salt, pepper, and Italian seasoning. Thread onto skewers.
3. **Grill:**
   - Grill skewers for 8-10 minutes, turning occasionally, until vegetables are tender and slightly charred.
4. **Serve:**
   - Serve warm as a side dish or main course.

## Spaghetti Squash with Marinara

### Ingredients

- 1 medium spaghetti squash
- 2 cups marinara sauce
- 1 tablespoon olive oil
- Salt and pepper to taste
- Grated Parmesan cheese (for topping, optional)
- Fresh basil (for garnish, optional)

### Instructions

1. **Cook Spaghetti Squash:**
    - Preheat the oven to 400°F (200°C). Cut the squash in half lengthwise, scoop out seeds, and drizzle with olive oil, salt, and pepper. Place cut-side down on a baking sheet. Bake for 40-45 minutes until tender.
2. **Prepare Marinara:**
    - Heat marinara sauce in a saucepan until warmed through.
3. **Scrape Squash:**
    - Once squash is cooked, use a fork to scrape out strands.
4. **Serve:**
    - Top spaghetti squash with marinara sauce, sprinkle with Parmesan, and garnish with fresh basil if desired.

Enjoy your delicious meals!

## Herb-Roasted Chicken Thighs

### Ingredients

- 4 bone-in, skin-on chicken thighs
- 2 tablespoons olive oil
- 2 teaspoons dried thyme
- 2 teaspoons dried rosemary
- 4 cloves garlic, minced
- Salt and pepper to taste
- 1 lemon, sliced

### Instructions

1. **Preheat the Oven:**
   - Preheat your oven to 425°F (220°C).
2. **Prepare the Chicken:**
   - In a bowl, mix olive oil, thyme, rosemary, garlic, salt, and pepper. Rub the mixture all over the chicken thighs.
3. **Arrange and Roast:**
   - Place chicken thighs in a baking dish and arrange lemon slices on top. Roast for 35-40 minutes or until the internal temperature reaches 165°F (75°C) and skin is crispy.
4. **Serve:**
   - Let rest for a few minutes before serving.

## Avocado and Tomato Salad

### Ingredients

- 2 ripe avocados, diced
- 2 cups cherry tomatoes, halved
- 1/4 red onion, finely chopped
- 2 tablespoons olive oil
- Juice of 1 lime
- Salt and pepper to taste
- Fresh cilantro or basil (for garnish, optional)

### Instructions

1. **Combine Ingredients:**
    - In a bowl, gently toss together avocados, cherry tomatoes, red onion, olive oil, lime juice, salt, and pepper.
2. **Garnish and Serve:**
    - Garnish with fresh herbs if desired. Serve immediately.

# Mushroom and Spinach Frittata

## Ingredients

- 6 large eggs
- 1 cup mushrooms, sliced
- 2 cups fresh spinach
- 1/2 cup milk
- 1/2 cup shredded cheese (cheddar or feta)
- Salt and pepper to taste
- 2 tablespoons olive oil

## Instructions

1. **Preheat the Oven:**
    - Preheat your oven to 350°F (175°C).
2. **Sauté Vegetables:**
    - In an oven-safe skillet, heat olive oil over medium heat. Add mushrooms and cook until softened. Stir in spinach and cook until wilted.
3. **Mix Eggs:**
    - In a bowl, whisk together eggs, milk, salt, and pepper. Pour over the sautéed vegetables and cook for a few minutes until edges start to set.
4. **Bake:**
    - Sprinkle cheese on top and transfer the skillet to the oven. Bake for 15-20 minutes until fully set.
5. **Serve:**
    - Let cool slightly before slicing and serving.

# Baked Tilapia with Lemon and Dill

## Ingredients

- 4 tilapia fillets
- 2 tablespoons olive oil
- Juice of 1 lemon
- 2 teaspoons fresh dill (or 1 teaspoon dried)
- Salt and pepper to taste
- Lemon slices (for garnish, optional)

## Instructions

1. **Preheat the Oven:**
   - Preheat your oven to 400°F (200°C).
2. **Prepare the Fillets:**
   - Place tilapia fillets on a baking sheet. Drizzle with olive oil and lemon juice, and sprinkle with dill, salt, and pepper.
3. **Bake:**
   - Bake for 12-15 minutes or until the fish flakes easily with a fork.
4. **Serve:**
   - Garnish with lemon slices and serve warm.

## Low-Carb Pizza with Cauliflower Crust

**Ingredients**

- 1 medium cauliflower, grated (about 2-3 cups)
- 1 cup shredded mozzarella cheese
- 1/4 cup grated Parmesan cheese
- 1 egg
- 1 teaspoon Italian seasoning
- Toppings of choice (pepperoni, veggies, etc.)

**Instructions**

1. **Preheat the Oven:**
    - Preheat your oven to 425°F (220°C).
2. **Prepare the Cauliflower:**
    - Steam or microwave grated cauliflower until soft. Let it cool, then squeeze out excess moisture using a clean towel.
3. **Make the Crust:**
    - In a bowl, mix cauliflower, mozzarella, Parmesan, egg, Italian seasoning, salt, and pepper. Spread mixture onto a baking sheet in a pizza shape.
4. **Bake the Crust:**
    - Bake for 15-20 minutes until golden brown.
5. **Add Toppings:**
    - Remove from oven, add toppings, and bake for an additional 10-15 minutes until cheese is melted.
6. **Serve:**
    - Slice and enjoy!

## Lentil and Vegetable Stew

### Ingredients

- 1 cup lentils (green or brown)
- 4 cups vegetable broth
- 1 onion, diced
- 2 carrots, diced
- 2 celery stalks, diced
- 2 cloves garlic, minced
- 1 can (14 oz) diced tomatoes
- 1 teaspoon thyme
- Salt and pepper to taste
- 2 cups kale or spinach (optional)

### Instructions

1. **Sauté Vegetables:**
    - In a large pot, sauté onion, carrots, and celery until softened. Add garlic and cook for another minute.
2. **Add Lentils and Broth:**
    - Stir in lentils, vegetable broth, diced tomatoes, thyme, salt, and pepper. Bring to a boil.
3. **Simmer:**
    - Reduce heat and simmer for 30-35 minutes until lentils are tender.
4. **Add Greens (Optional):**
    - Stir in kale or spinach and cook for another 5 minutes.
5. **Serve:**
    - Enjoy warm with crusty bread or on its own.

Enjoy your delicious meals!

# Greek Salad with Grilled Chicken

## Ingredients

- 4 cups mixed greens
- 1 cup cherry tomatoes, halved
- 1 cucumber, diced
- 1/2 red onion, thinly sliced
- 1/2 cup Kalamata olives, pitted and halved
- 1 cup feta cheese, crumbled
- 2 grilled chicken breasts, sliced
- 2 tablespoons olive oil
- Juice of 1 lemon
- Salt and pepper to taste
- Dried oregano (for garnish, optional)

## Instructions

1. **Prepare the Salad:**
    - In a large bowl, combine mixed greens, cherry tomatoes, cucumber, red onion, olives, and feta cheese.
2. **Add Chicken:**
    - Top the salad with sliced grilled chicken.
3. **Dress the Salad:**
    - In a small bowl, whisk together olive oil, lemon juice, salt, and pepper. Drizzle over the salad.
4. **Serve:**
    - Toss gently and garnish with oregano if desired.

# Coconut Flour Muffins

## Ingredients

- 1/2 cup coconut flour
- 1/4 cup honey or maple syrup
- 4 large eggs
- 1/2 cup coconut milk
- 1/4 cup melted coconut oil
- 1 teaspoon baking powder
- 1/2 teaspoon vanilla extract
- 1/4 teaspoon salt

## Instructions

1. **Preheat the Oven:**
   - Preheat your oven to 350°F (175°C) and line a muffin tin with liners.
2. **Mix Ingredients:**
   - In a bowl, whisk together coconut flour, baking powder, and salt. In another bowl, combine eggs, honey, coconut milk, melted coconut oil, and vanilla.
3. **Combine and Pour:**
   - Mix the wet ingredients into the dry ingredients until smooth. Pour the batter into the prepared muffin tin.
4. **Bake:**
   - Bake for 18-20 minutes or until a toothpick comes out clean.
5. **Serve:**
   - Let cool before serving.

**Cabbage Roll Casserole**

**Ingredients**

- 1 pound ground beef or turkey
- 1 onion, diced
- 1 head cabbage, chopped
- 2 cups tomato sauce
- 1 cup cooked rice (or cauliflower rice)
- 1 teaspoon garlic powder
- 1 teaspoon paprika
- Salt and pepper to taste
- 1 tablespoon olive oil

**Instructions**

1. **Preheat the Oven:**
   - Preheat your oven to 350°F (175°C).
2. **Sauté Meat and Onion:**
   - In a skillet, heat olive oil over medium heat. Add onion and cook until soft. Add ground beef or turkey, cooking until browned.
3. **Add Cabbage:**
   - Stir in chopped cabbage, cooking until wilted. Add tomato sauce, cooked rice, garlic powder, paprika, salt, and pepper. Mix well.
4. **Bake:**
   - Transfer the mixture to a baking dish and bake for 30-35 minutes until heated through.
5. **Serve:**
   - Let cool slightly before serving.

# Berry Smoothie with Spinach

## Ingredients

- 1 cup spinach
- 1 cup mixed berries (fresh or frozen)
- 1 banana
- 1 cup almond milk (or any milk of choice)
- 1 tablespoon honey or maple syrup (optional)
- 1 tablespoon chia seeds (optional)

## Instructions

1. **Blend Ingredients:**
    - In a blender, combine spinach, berries, banana, almond milk, honey, and chia seeds.
2. **Blend Until Smooth:**
    - Blend until smooth and creamy. Adjust thickness with more milk if desired.
3. **Serve:**
    - Pour into a glass and enjoy immediately.

## Oven-Baked Falafel

**Ingredients**

- 1 can (15 oz) chickpeas, rinsed and drained
- 1/4 cup onion, chopped
- 2 cloves garlic
- 2 tablespoons fresh parsley, chopped
- 2 tablespoons fresh cilantro, chopped
- 1 teaspoon cumin
- 1 teaspoon coriander
- Salt and pepper to taste
- 2 tablespoons olive oil

**Instructions**

1. **Preheat the Oven:**
   - Preheat your oven to 400°F (200°C) and line a baking sheet with parchment paper.
2. **Blend Ingredients:**
   - In a food processor, combine chickpeas, onion, garlic, parsley, cilantro, cumin, coriander, salt, and pepper. Pulse until a coarse mixture forms.
3. **Form Balls:**
   - Shape the mixture into small balls and place them on the prepared baking sheet. Drizzle with olive oil.
4. **Bake:**
   - Bake for 25-30 minutes, flipping halfway through, until golden brown.
5. **Serve:**
   - Serve warm with tahini sauce or yogurt.

## Almond-Crusted Chicken Tenders

**Ingredients**

- 1 pound chicken tenders
- 1 cup almond flour
- 1 teaspoon garlic powder
- 1 teaspoon paprika
- Salt and pepper to taste
- 2 large eggs, beaten
- 1 tablespoon olive oil (for drizzling)

**Instructions**

1. **Preheat the Oven:**
   - Preheat your oven to 400°F (200°C) and line a baking sheet with parchment paper.
2. **Prepare Coating:**
   - In a shallow bowl, mix almond flour, garlic powder, paprika, salt, and pepper.
3. **Coat Chicken:**
   - Dip each chicken tender in beaten eggs, then coat with the almond flour mixture. Place on the prepared baking sheet.
4. **Bake:**
   - Drizzle with olive oil and bake for 20-25 minutes until golden brown and cooked through.
5. **Serve:**
   - Serve warm with your favorite dipping sauce.

Enjoy your delicious meals!

# Roasted Brussels Sprouts with Balsamic

## Ingredients

- 1 pound Brussels sprouts, halved
- 2 tablespoons olive oil
- Salt and pepper to taste
- 1/4 cup balsamic vinegar
- 1 tablespoon honey (optional)

## Instructions

1. **Preheat the Oven:**
   - Preheat your oven to 400°F (200°C).
2. **Prepare Brussels Sprouts:**
   - Toss halved Brussels sprouts with olive oil, salt, and pepper. Spread on a baking sheet in a single layer.
3. **Roast:**
   - Roast for 20-25 minutes, stirring halfway through, until tender and caramelized.
4. **Glaze:**
   - In the last 5 minutes, drizzle with balsamic vinegar and honey (if using) and return to the oven.
5. **Serve:**
   - Serve warm as a side dish.

# Curried Quinoa and Vegetable Bowl

## Ingredients

- 1 cup quinoa, rinsed
- 2 cups vegetable broth or water
- 1 tablespoon curry powder
- 1 cup mixed vegetables (carrots, peas, bell peppers)
- 1 tablespoon olive oil
- Salt and pepper to taste
- Fresh cilantro (for garnish)

## Instructions

1. **Cook Quinoa:**
    - In a pot, combine quinoa, vegetable broth, curry powder, salt, and pepper. Bring to a boil, then reduce heat and simmer for 15 minutes until quinoa is cooked.
2. **Sauté Vegetables:**
    - In a skillet, heat olive oil over medium heat. Add mixed vegetables and sauté until tender.
3. **Combine:**
    - Fluff quinoa with a fork and mix in sautéed vegetables.
4. **Serve:**
    - Garnish with fresh cilantro and serve warm.

## Zesty Lemon Garlic Shrimp

**Ingredients**

- 1 pound shrimp, peeled and deveined
- 3 tablespoons olive oil
- 4 cloves garlic, minced
- Juice of 1 lemon
- 1 teaspoon lemon zest
- Salt and pepper to taste
- Fresh parsley (for garnish)

**Instructions**

1. **Sauté Garlic:**
   - In a skillet, heat olive oil over medium heat. Add garlic and sauté until fragrant.
2. **Cook Shrimp:**
   - Add shrimp, lemon juice, lemon zest, salt, and pepper. Cook for 3-4 minutes until shrimp are pink and cooked through.
3. **Serve:**
   - Garnish with fresh parsley and serve immediately.

## Apple Cinnamon Overnight Oats

### Ingredients

- 1 cup rolled oats
- 1 cup almond milk (or any milk of choice)
- 1 apple, diced
- 1 teaspoon cinnamon
- 1 tablespoon honey or maple syrup (optional)
- 1/4 cup walnuts or almonds (optional)

### Instructions

1. **Combine Ingredients:**
    - In a jar or bowl, mix rolled oats, almond milk, diced apple, cinnamon, and sweetener if using.
2. **Refrigerate:**
    - Cover and refrigerate overnight.
3. **Serve:**
    - In the morning, top with nuts if desired and enjoy!

# Beef and Broccoli Stir-Fry

## Ingredients

- 1 pound beef sirloin, sliced thin
- 3 cups broccoli florets
- 2 tablespoons soy sauce
- 1 tablespoon oyster sauce (optional)
- 2 cloves garlic, minced
- 1 tablespoon cornstarch
- 2 tablespoons vegetable oil

## Instructions

1. **Marinate Beef:**
    - Toss beef with soy sauce, oyster sauce, and cornstarch. Let marinate for 15 minutes.
2. **Sauté Broccoli:**
    - In a skillet, heat 1 tablespoon of vegetable oil over medium-high heat. Add broccoli and cook until tender. Remove and set aside.
3. **Cook Beef:**
    - In the same skillet, add remaining oil and cook marinated beef until browned. Add garlic and sauté for an additional minute.
4. **Combine:**
    - Return broccoli to the skillet, tossing everything together.
5. **Serve:**
    - Serve hot over rice or noodles.

## Cilantro Lime Rice with Black Beans

### Ingredients

- 1 cup rice (white or brown)
- 2 cups water
- 1 can (15 oz) black beans, rinsed and drained
- Juice of 1 lime
- 1/4 cup fresh cilantro, chopped
- Salt to taste

### Instructions

1. **Cook Rice:**
   - In a pot, bring water to a boil. Add rice, cover, and simmer according to package instructions.
2. **Mix Ingredients:**
   - Once rice is cooked, fluff with a fork and stir in black beans, lime juice, cilantro, and salt.
3. **Serve:**
   - Serve warm as a side dish or base for a bowl.

**Creamy Avocado Dressing Salad**

**Ingredients**

- 1 ripe avocado
- 1/4 cup Greek yogurt or sour cream
- 2 tablespoons olive oil
- Juice of 1 lime
- 1 clove garlic
- Salt and pepper to taste
- Mixed greens or salad of choice

**Instructions**

1. **Make Dressing:**
    - In a blender, combine avocado, Greek yogurt, olive oil, lime juice, garlic, salt, and pepper. Blend until smooth.
2. **Prepare Salad:**
    - Toss mixed greens with the avocado dressing until well coated.
3. **Serve:**
    - Enjoy immediately as a fresh side or main dish.

Enjoy your delicious meals!

## Herb-Crusted Baked Cod

**Ingredients**

- 4 cod fillets
- 1/2 cup breadcrumbs
- 2 tablespoons olive oil
- 2 tablespoons fresh parsley, chopped
- 1 tablespoon fresh dill, chopped
- 1 lemon, zested
- Salt and pepper to taste

**Instructions**

1. **Preheat the Oven:**
    - Preheat your oven to 400°F (200°C).
2. **Prepare the Topping:**
    - In a bowl, mix breadcrumbs, olive oil, parsley, dill, lemon zest, salt, and pepper.
3. **Coat Cod:**
    - Place cod fillets on a baking sheet and top each with the breadcrumb mixture.
4. **Bake:**
    - Bake for 15-20 minutes until the fish is flaky and the topping is golden brown.
5. **Serve:**
    - Serve warm with lemon wedges.

# Spiced Chickpeas and Spinach

## Ingredients

- 1 can (15 oz) chickpeas, rinsed and drained
- 2 cups fresh spinach
- 2 tablespoons olive oil
- 1 teaspoon cumin
- 1 teaspoon smoked paprika
- Salt and pepper to taste
- 1 clove garlic, minced

## Instructions

1. **Sauté Chickpeas:**
   - In a skillet, heat olive oil over medium heat. Add chickpeas, cumin, smoked paprika, salt, pepper, and garlic. Cook for about 5 minutes until chickpeas are heated through.
2. **Add Spinach:**
   - Stir in fresh spinach and cook until wilted.
3. **Serve:**
   - Serve warm as a side or main dish.

# Green Bean Almondine

## Ingredients

- 1 pound green beans, trimmed
- 1/4 cup sliced almonds
- 2 tablespoons butter
- 1 tablespoon lemon juice
- Salt and pepper to taste

## Instructions

1. **Blanch Green Beans:**
   - Bring a pot of salted water to a boil. Add green beans and blanch for 3-4 minutes. Drain and rinse under cold water.
2. **Sauté Almonds:**
   - In a skillet, melt butter over medium heat. Add sliced almonds and toast until golden.
3. **Combine:**
   - Add green beans to the skillet and drizzle with lemon juice, salt, and pepper. Toss to combine.
4. **Serve:**
   - Serve warm as a side dish.

# Low-Sugar Chocolate Avocado Mousse

## Ingredients

- 2 ripe avocados
- 1/4 cup unsweetened cocoa powder
- 1/4 cup almond milk (or milk of choice)
- 1/4 cup maple syrup or sweetener of choice
- 1 teaspoon vanilla extract
- Pinch of salt

## Instructions

1. **Blend Ingredients:**
    - In a blender or food processor, combine avocados, cocoa powder, almond milk, maple syrup, vanilla, and salt. Blend until smooth and creamy.
2. **Chill:**
    - Transfer to serving dishes and refrigerate for at least 30 minutes.
3. **Serve:**
    - Serve chilled, optionally topped with berries.

# Baked Acorn Squash with Cinnamon

## Ingredients

- 1 acorn squash, halved and seeded
- 2 tablespoons butter or coconut oil
- 2 tablespoons brown sugar or maple syrup
- 1 teaspoon cinnamon
- Salt to taste

## Instructions

1. **Preheat the Oven:**
   - Preheat your oven to 400°F (200°C).
2. **Prepare Squash:**
   - Place acorn squash halves cut-side up on a baking sheet. Dot with butter, sprinkle with brown sugar, cinnamon, and salt.
3. **Bake:**
   - Bake for 40-45 minutes until tender.
4. **Serve:**
   - Serve warm as a side dish.

# Spicy Roasted Cauliflower

## Ingredients

- 1 head cauliflower, cut into florets
- 2 tablespoons olive oil
- 1 teaspoon chili powder
- 1 teaspoon cumin
- Salt and pepper to taste

## Instructions

1. **Preheat the Oven:**
   - Preheat your oven to 425°F (220°C).
2. **Toss Cauliflower:**
   - In a bowl, toss cauliflower florets with olive oil, chili powder, cumin, salt, and pepper.
3. **Roast:**
   - Spread on a baking sheet and roast for 25-30 minutes until golden and tender.
4. **Serve:**
   - Serve warm as a side dish.

# Mediterranean Stuffed Zucchini

## Ingredients

- 2 medium zucchinis, halved lengthwise
- 1 cup cooked quinoa or rice
- 1/2 cup cherry tomatoes, halved
- 1/4 cup feta cheese, crumbled
- 2 tablespoons olives, chopped
- 1 tablespoon olive oil
- Salt and pepper to taste

## Instructions

1. **Preheat the Oven:**
    - Preheat your oven to 375°F (190°C).
2. **Prepare Zucchini:**
    - Scoop out the center of each zucchini half to create boats. Drizzle with olive oil and season with salt and pepper.
3. **Mix Filling:**
    - In a bowl, combine quinoa, cherry tomatoes, feta cheese, olives, salt, and pepper.
4. **Stuff and Bake:**
    - Fill zucchini halves with the mixture and place on a baking sheet. Bake for 25-30 minutes until zucchini is tender.
5. **Serve:**
    - Serve warm as a main or side dish.

## Grilled Eggplant with Tomato Sauce

**Ingredients**

- 1 large eggplant, sliced into rounds
- 2 tablespoons olive oil
- Salt and pepper to taste
- 2 cups marinara sauce
- 1/4 cup fresh basil, chopped

**Instructions**

1. **Preheat the Grill:**
    - Preheat your grill to medium heat.
2. **Prepare Eggplant:**
    - Brush eggplant slices with olive oil and season with salt and pepper.
3. **Grill:**
    - Grill eggplant for 4-5 minutes per side until tender and charred.
4. **Serve:**
    - Top grilled eggplant with warm marinara sauce and garnish with fresh basil.

Enjoy your delicious meals!

## Raspberry Chia Jam

### Ingredients

- 2 cups fresh or frozen raspberries
- 2 tablespoons honey or maple syrup (optional)
- 3 tablespoons chia seeds
- 1 teaspoon vanilla extract (optional)

### Instructions

1. **Cook Raspberries:**
   - In a small saucepan over medium heat, combine the raspberries and honey (if using). Cook for about 5-7 minutes, stirring occasionally until the raspberries break down and release their juices.
2. **Add Chia Seeds:**
   - Remove the saucepan from heat and stir in chia seeds and vanilla extract (if using). Mix well.
3. **Let it Set:**
   - Allow the mixture to sit for about 10-15 minutes. The chia seeds will absorb the liquid and thicken the jam.
4. **Store:**
   - Transfer to a clean jar and refrigerate. The jam will keep for about 1-2 weeks.
5. **Serve:**
   - Enjoy on toast, yogurt, or as a topping for desserts!

## Nutty Granola Bars (Low-Sugar)

**Ingredients**

- 1 1/2 cups rolled oats
- 1/2 cup nut butter (almond, peanut, or sunflower)
- 1/4 cup honey or maple syrup
- 1/2 cup mixed nuts (chopped)
- 1/4 cup seeds (pumpkin, sunflower, or flax)
- 1/4 teaspoon salt
- 1/2 teaspoon vanilla extract (optional)

**Instructions**

1. **Preheat the Oven:**
    - Preheat your oven to 350°F (175°C) and line an 8x8 inch baking dish with parchment paper.
2. **Mix Ingredients:**
    - In a large bowl, combine rolled oats, nut butter, honey, mixed nuts, seeds, salt, and vanilla extract. Mix until well combined.
3. **Press into Dish:**
    - Pour the mixture into the prepared baking dish and press it down firmly into an even layer.
4. **Bake:**
    - Bake for 15-20 minutes, or until the edges are golden brown.
5. **Cool and Cut:**
    - Allow to cool completely in the pan before lifting out and cutting into bars.
6. **Store:**
    - Store in an airtight container for up to a week.

Enjoy your delicious homemade treats!